MARY
Cassatt

Paintings

WINGS BOOKS
New York • Avenel, New Jersey

Copyright © 1993 by Outlet Book Company, Inc.

This 1993 edition is published by Wings Books,
distributed by Outlet Book Company, Inc.,
a Random House Company,
40 Engelhard Avenue, Avenel, New Jersey 07001.

Random House
New York • Toronto • London • Sydney • Auckland

Grateful acknowledgment is made to Art Resource and Superstock
for permission to use their transparencies of the artwork.

Printed and bound in Malaysia

Library of Congress Cataloging-in-Publication Data

Cassatt, Mary, 1844-1926.
    Mary Cassatt : paintings.
       p.   cm.
    Includes bibliographical references.
    ISBN 0-517-09355-3
    1. Cassatt, Mary, 1844-1926 – Catalogs. I. Title.
ND1329.C38A4 1993
759. 13 – dc20

                                       93-3826
                                        CIP
                                        AC

8 7 6 5 4 3 2 1

"In art what we want is the certainty that one spark of original genius shall not be extinguished." [1]

—MARY CASSATT

1. *Mother and Child*

2. *Bust of a Girl*

3. *Spanish Dancer Wearing a Lace Mantilla* 1873

4. *Head of a Little Girl*

5. *Young Woman Sewing in a Garden* c.1886

6. *Little Girl in a Blue Armchair* 1878

7. *Sara in a Green Bonnet* c.1901

8. *The Caress* 1902

9. *Margot in White*

10. *Reading "Le Figaro"* c.1878

11. *Five O'Clock Tea 1880*

12. *The Child's Caress*

13. *Susan on a Balcony Holding a Dog* 1883

14. *In the Garden 1904*

15. *Child Drinking*

16. *Family Group Reading* c.1905

17. *Vase of Lilacs at the Window*

18. *Summertime* 1894

19. *Mother and Child*

20. *Portrait of Helen Sears*

21. *The Loge* 1882

22. *Mother About to Wash her Sleepy Child 1880*

23. *Woman Reading*

24. *Anne–Marie Durand–Ruel*

25. *The Boating Party* 1894

26. *Antoinette at her Dressing Table 1909*

27. *Grandmother Reading to her Grandchildren* 1880

28. *Mother and Child*

Afterword

A proper Victorian woman, she joined one of the most revolutionary groups of artists the world has ever known; an American, she was greatly esteemed by the French and received the coveted Legion of Honor; unmarried and childless, she created quintessential portraits of maternity.

Mary Cassatt, born in 1844 in Pittsburgh, enjoyed a privileged childhood, including several years in Europe with her family. When the family returned, settling in Philadelphia, Cassatt in 1860 entered the Pennsylvania Academy of Fine Arts, America's most prestigious art school. After two years of study and much independent work, Cassatt realized that to pursue a career as a painter, she would have to study the old masters. She returned to Europe in 1865, first working in Charles Chaplin's Paris studio, and later joining the artist colony in the Forest of Fountainbleu. She learned her lessons well: *The Mandolin Player*, a portrait in the 17th-century realist style, was accepted for the 1868 Salon Exhibition in Paris—an extraordinary accomplishment for a beginning artist.

Although she returned to the United States in 1870 at the outbreak of the Franco-Prussian War, by the end of 1871 Cassatt was back in Europe, this time in Italy. Her studies there of Correggio and other Italian masters had a lasting effect, both on Cassatt's penchant for classical composition and her adoption of the Madonna and Child as a prevalent theme in her paintings. She also studied the works of Flemish and Spanish masters; her appreciation of Velasquez can be readily seen in *Spanish Dancer Wearing a Lace Mantilla* (plate 3).

In 1874, Cassatt settled in Paris. She later reflected on the event which changed her life: "How well I remember seeing for the first time Degas' pastels in the window of a picture dealer...I used to go and flatten my nose against that window and absorb all I could of his art."[2] It was Degas who, after a visit to her studio in 1877, swept Cassatt into the circle of Impressionists; their friendship would last a lifetime. Although she continued to be exhibited by the official Salon, Cassatt's identification with the Impressionists was immediate: "I recognized my true masters. I admired Manet, Courbet, and Degas. I hated conventional art. Now I began to live."[3] The impact of Manet and Degas can be seen in Cassatt's use of strong, clear colors in *The Loge* (plate 21), one of eleven Cassatt works shown in the Impressionist Exhibition of 1879 that marked Cassatt's entry into the group of self-declared "Independents."

Cassatt retained her ties with America; her paintings at the Pennsylvania Academy of Fine Arts Annual in 1876, 1878, and 1879, and at the Annual Exhibition of the National Academy of Design in New York in 1878, were the first Impressionist works to be exhibited in the United States.[4] Moreover, as a result of her friendship with Louisine Elder Havermeyer and other wealthy Americans, Cassatt became an advisor to American art buyers in Paris, encouraging them to purchase Impressionist works.

During the late 1870s and early 1880s, in works like *Woman Reading* (plate 23), Cassatt adapted Impressionist techniques without abandoning the more formal draftsmanship she had learned from her studies of traditional painters. The asymmetry and use of empty space in *Little Girl in a Blue Armchair* (plate 6) shows her debt to Degas—in fact, Degas helped Cassatt paint the background of the picture. *Reading "Le Figaro"* (plate 10) is another superb example of the balance between classic composition and Impressionist style that is characteristic of Cassatt's works of this period. This realistic representation of an everyday scene—Cassatt's own mother posed for the painting—won critical acclaim. When it was exhibited at the Society of American Artists in New York, S.N. Carter wrote:

> It is pleasant to see how well an ordinary person dressed in an ordinary way can be made to look...we think nobody seeing this lady reading...could have failed to like the well-drawn, well-lighted, well-atomized, and well-composed painting.[5]

Experimenting with surface effects, color, and light in the Impressionist manner, Cassatt also followed their lead in subject matter. The motif that would bring her work acclaim throughout her career—young women and children in relaxed poses—embodied her belief that painters should depict the world around them. The delightful *Mother About to Wash her Sleepy Child* (plate 22) is generally regarded as Cassatt's first comprehensive treatment of the mother-and-child theme.[6] Although her contemporaries employed similar subjects, Cassatt brought a different sensibility to her portraits. In exploring women in their own settings—nurseries, gardens, living rooms—Cassatt, an adamant believer in women's independence, conveys an introspective, emotional quality—an *understanding*—not found in works by Renoir or Degas.

Divided by artistic and personal conflicts, the Impressionists mounted their last group exhibition in 1886. Cassatt had already begun turning away from many of their precepts, returning to a more classical emphasis on form, precision, and structure. An exhibition of Japanese prints in Paris in 1890 had a profound effect on Cassatt's work, especially apparent in the clear outlines and use of color patterns in her subsequent works. Her magnificent colored engravings—the centerpiece of her first solo exhibit at the Durand-Ruel gallery in April 1891—show this influence, as do the oils *Young Woman Sewing in a Garden* (plate 5) and *The Caress* (plate 8).

The exhibit at Durand-Ruel firmly established Cassatt's independence from the Impressionist group, and demonstrated that a woman—and an American at that—could command attention in the male-dominated French art circles. Eager to make a name for herself in her own country, Cassatt accepted a commission to paint a mural for the Woman's Building at the 1893 Exposition in Chicago. Here, too, her concern was with depicting women through a woman's eyes:

> I have tried to express the modern woman in the fashions of our day....Men I have no doubt are painted in all their vigor on the walls of other buildings; to us the sweetness of childhood, the charm of womanhood, if I have not conveyed some sense of that charm, in one word if I have not been absolutely feminine, then I have failed.[7]

Throughout the 1890s, Cassatt pursued new artistic directions. Larger in scale than her previous paintings, *The Boating Party* (plate 25) is almost Van Gogh-like in its impact: the bold colors and severe foreshortening turn the boat and the sail into almost abstract shapes. This painting suggests that Cassatt was striving for a new emotional effect as well: while the intimacy of the mother and child echoes Cassatt's other works, the presence of a male figure adds an unusual ambiguity to this depiction of a family outing. *Summertime* (plate 18), also painted in 1894, shows an increasing freedom in Cassatt's oil techniques. This new freedom is carried into Cassatt's work of the first decade of the twentieth century. Though the composition of *Young Mother Sewing* (front cover) is still fairly formal, the paint is applied in thick, sweeping brushstrokes. With its figures casually placed in an outdoor setting, *Family Group Reading* (plate 16) represents Cassatt's successful experiment with the extension of space and the relaxation of formal structure; it is imbued with a naturalism not found in Cassatt's earlier works.

Toward the end of her life, Cassatt became isolated and bitter[8]; she neither understood nor liked "modern" art. Taken to an open house at Gertrude and Leo Stein's in 1908, Cassatt looked at a dozen early Picassos and Matisses and announced, "I have never seen so many dreadful paintings in one place; I have never seen so many dreadful people gathered together...."[9] The onset of blindness in 1915 brought her career as a painter to a close; she died on June 14, 1926 in her small chateau in Mensil-Theribus.

In 1893, ninety-eight of Cassatt's works were exhibited in Durand-Ruel's gallery, an indication of her acceptance by critics and collectors alike. Two years later, in his newly opened gallery in New York, Durand-Ruel mounted Cassatt's first individual exhibit in her homeland. It was not until several years later, however, that the American art establishment would recognize the importance of their "native daughter." Cassatt's last visit to America in 1899 went virtually unnoticed in the press. Finally, in 1904, the Pennsylvania Academy awarded her the Lippincott Prize for *The Caress*. Cassatt refused the award, writing to the Managing Director of the

Academy, "I...who belong to the founders of the Independent Exhibition must stick to my principles, our principles, which were, no jury, no medals, no awards."[10] That same year, she was made a *chevalier de la legion d'honneur* in France, the most coveted honor of her profession. In 1914, Cassatt accepted the Gold Medal of Honor from the Pennsylvania Academy of Art since it honored her general contributions to art, not one picture.

The recognition Cassatt long sought in America ironically bloomed in the years following her death. Today, she is known as America's best woman painter. But her contributions to art extend beyond gender or nationality. As Watson Forbes wrote, "Much more interesting would be a list of men who painted better than Mary. It would be a very short list."[11]

NOTES

1. Sophia Craze, *Mary Cassatt* (New York: Crescent Books), 7
2. Jay Roudebush, *Mary Cassatt* (New York: Crown Publishers), 13
3. Frederick A. Sweet, *Miss Mary Cassatt* (Norman:University of Oklahoma Press), 211
4. Hugo Munsterberg, *A History of Women Artists* (New York: Clarkson Potter), 57
5. Craze, 27
6. Roudebush, 38
7. Sweet, 130-131
8. Munsterberg, 57
9. Ibid, 59
10. Sweet, 165
11. Nancy Hale, *Mary Cassatt* (Reading: Addison-Wesley Publishing Company), 285

List of Plates

The photographs in this book were supplied by: